SPANISH
Made Nice & Easy!®

Staff of Research & Education Association
Carl Fuchs, Language Program Director

Based on Language Courses developed by the
U.S. Government for Foreign Service Personnel

Research & Education Association
Visit our website at
www.rea.com

Research & Education Association
61 Ethel Road West
Piscataway, New Jersey 08854
E-mail: info@rea.com

SPANISH MADE NICE & EASY®

Published 2008

Printed in the United States of America

Library of Congress Control Number 00-193033

ISBN-13: 978-0-87891-377-0
ISBN-10: 0-87891-377-7

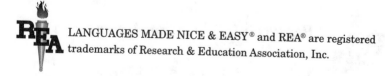

What This Guide Will Do For You

Whether travelling to a foreign country or to your favorite international restaurant, this *Nice & Easy* guide gives you just enough of the language to get around and be understood. Much of the material in this book was developed for government personnel who are often assigned to a foreign country on a moment's notice and need a quick introduction to the language.

In this handy and compact guide, you will find useful words and phrases, popular expressions, common greetings, and the words for numbers, money, and time. Every word or phrase is accompanied with the correct pronunciation and spelling. There is a vocabulary list for finding words quickly.

Generous margins on the pages allow you to make notes and remarks that you may find helpful.

If you expect to travel to Spain, the section on the country's history and relevant up-to-date facts will make your trip more informative and enjoyable. By keeping this guide with you, you'll be well prepared to understand as well as converse in Spanish.

Carl Fuchs
Language Program Director

Contents

Spain

Facts & History

Official Name: Kingdom of Spain

Geography

Area: 504,750 sq. km. (194,884 sq. mi.), including the Balearic and Canary Islands; about the size of Arizona and Utah combined.

Cities: *Capital*—Madrid (pop. 3.0 million est). *Other cities*—Barcelona (5.0 million), Valencia (3.8 million), Seville (1.8 million), Zaragoza (620,000), Bilbao (358,000), Malaga (528,000).

Terrain: High plateaus and mountains.

People

Nationality: *Noun*—Spaniard(s). *Adjective*—Spanish.

Population: 45 million est.

Annual growth rate: 0.6%.

Ethnic groups: Distinct ethnic groups within Spain include the Basques, Catalans, and Galicians. Spain's population density, lower than that of most European countries, is roughly equivalent to New England's. In recent years, following a longstanding pattern in the rest of Europe, rural populations are moving to cities. Religion: Predominantly Roman Catholic. Spain has no official religion. The constitution of 1978 disestablished the Roman Catholic Church as the official state religion, while recognizing the role it plays in Spanish society. More than 90% of the population are at least nominally Catholic.

Languages: Spanish (official), Catalan-Valenciana 17%, Galician 7%, Basque 2%.

Education: *Years compulsory*—to age 16. *Literacy*—97%.

Work force: (16.2 million): *Services*—61%; *agriculture*—8%; *construction*—9.8%; *industry*—17.6%.

Government

Type: Constitutional monarchy (Juan Carlos I proclaimed King November 22, 1975).

Constitution: 1978

Branches: *Executive*—President of government nominated by monarch.

Legislative—Cortes: a 350-seat Congress of Deputies (elected by the d'Hondt system of proportional representation) and a Senate. *Judicial*—Constitutional Tribunal has jurisdiction over constitutional issues. Supreme Tribunal heads system comprising territorial, provincial, regional, and municipal courts.

History of Spain

One of the characteristic features of the early history of Spain is the successive waves of different peoples who spread all over the peninsula. The first to appear were the Iberians, a Libyan people, who came from the south. Later came the Celts, a typically Aryan people, and from the merging of the two there arose a new race, the Celtiberians, who divided into several tribes (Cantabrians, Asturians, Lusitanians) and gave their names to their respective homelands. The next to arrive, attracted by mining wealth, were the Phoenicians, who founded a number of trading posts along the coast, the most important being that of Cadiz. After this came Greek settlers, who founded several towns, including Rosas, Ampurias, and Sagunto. The Phoenicians, in their struggle against the Greeks, called on the Carthaginians, who, under the orders of Hamilcar Barca, took possession of most of Spain. It was at this time that Rome raised a border dispute in defense of the areas of Greek influence, and thus began in the peninsula the Second Punic War, which decided the fate of the world at that time. After the Roman victory, Publius Cornelius Scipio, Africanus, began the conquest of Spain, which was to be under Roman rule for six centuries.

Once the peninsula had been completely subdued,

it was Romanized to such an extent that it produced writers of the stature of Seneca and Lucan and such eminent emperors as Trajan and Hadrian. Rome left in Spain four powerful social elements: the Latin language, Roman law, the municipality, and the Christian religion. After the fall of the Roman Empire, the Suevi, Vandals, and Alans entered Spain, but they were defeated by the Visigoths who, by the end of the 6th century, had occupied virtually the whole of the peninsula. At the beginning of the 8th century the Arabs entered from the south. They conquered the country swiftly except for a small bulwark in the north which would become the initial springboard for the Reconquest, which was not completed until eight centuries later. The period of Muslim sway is divided into three periods: the Emirate (711 to 756), the Caliphate (756-1031) and the Reinos de Taifas (small independent kingdoms,1031 to 1492).

In 1469, the marriage of the Catholic monarchs, Isabella of Castile and Ferdinand of Aragon, prepared the way for the union of the two kingdoms and marked the opening of a period of growing success for Spain. During their reign, Granada, the last stronghold of the Arabs in Spain, was conquered and in the same historic year of 1492, the caravels sent by the Crown of Castile under the command of Christopher Columbus discovered America. The Canary Islands became part of Spanish territory (1495); the hegemony of Spain in the Mediterranean, to the detriment of France, was affirmed with the conquest of the Kingdom of Naples; and Navarre was incorporated into the Kingdom.

The next two centuries, the 16th and the 17th, witnessed the construction and apogee of the Spanish Empire as a result of which the country, under the aegis of the Austrians, became the world's foremost power, and European politics hinged upon it.

The War of Succession to the Spanish Crown (1701-1714) marked the end of the dynasty of the Hapsburgs and the coming of the Bourbons. The Treaty of Utrecht in 1713 formalized the British occupation of the Rock of Gibraltar, giving rise to an anachronistic colonial situation which still persists today and constitutes the only dispute between Spain and the United Kingdom. In 1808, following the Napoleonic invasion, Joseph Bonaparte was installed on the Spanish throne, although the fierce resistance of the Spanish people culminated in the restoration of the Bourbons in the person of Fernando VII. The history of the rest of the 19th century was dominated by the dynastic dilemma produced by the death without male heir of Ferdinand VII. His daughter took the throne as Isabel II, but her uncle, the legendary Don Carlos, opposed her claim. This gave rise to the first of the two Carlist Wars, which chiefly affected Navarre, the Basque Country and El Maestrazgo, the region which bestrides Castellon, Tarragona and Teruel.

When the Spanish diplomats attended the Congress of Vienna in 1814, they represented a victorious State, but a ruined and divided nation. The profound crisis of Spain had seriously undermined the Spanish American empire because many of the American colonies claimed their independence in the first decades of the 19th century. In 1873, the brief reign of Amadeo of Savoy ended with his abdication, and the First Republic was proclaimed. However, a military pronunciamiento in 1875 restored the monarchy and Alfonso XII was proclaimed King of Spain. He was succeeded in 1886 by his son Alfonso XIII, although his mother, Queen Maria Cristina of Habsburg acted as regent until 1902, when he was crowned king. Prior to this, a brief war with the United States resulted in the loss of Cuba, Puerto Rico, and the Philippines in 1898, thus completing the dissolution of the Spanish overseas empire.

Spain remained neutral in the First World War. Primo de Rivera's dictatorship solved some of the multiple problems plaguing the country: he ended the war in Africa, developed local governments and presented an ambitious public works program. However, the attempt to return to a constitutional government by integrating a consultative National Assembly

(1926) failed with the rejection of the Drafts of the Constitution of the Spanish Monarchy (1929).

In the municipal elections of 1931, it became clear that in all the large towns of Spain the candidates who supported the Monarchy had been heavily defeated. The size of the Republican vote in cities such as Madrid and Barcelona was enormous. In the country districts the Monarchy gained enough seats to secure a majority in the nation as a whole. But it was well known that in the country the "caciques" were still powerful enough to prevent a fair vote. By the evening of the day following the elections, great crowds were gathering in the streets of Madrid. The king's most trusted friends advised him to leave the capital without delay to prevent bloodshed. As a result, Alfonso XIII left Spain and the Second Republic was established. During its five-year lifetime, it was ridden with all kinds of political, economic and social, conflicts, which inexorably split opinions into two irreconcilable sides. The climate of growing violence culminated on July 18, 1936 in a military rising which turned into a tragic civil war that did not end until three years later.

On October 1, 1936, General Franco took over as Head of State and Commander-in-Chief of the Armed Forces. The Spanish State embarked on a period of forty years' dictatorship, during which the political life of the country was characterized by the illegality of all the political parties except the National Movement. Franco died in 1975, bringing to an end a period of Spanish history and opening the way to the restoration of the monarchy with the rise to the throne of the present King of Spain, Juan Carlos I de Borbon y Borbon.

The young monarch soon established himself as a resolute motor for change to a western-style democracy by means of a cautious process of political reform which took as its starting point the Francoist legal structure. Adolfo Suarez, the prime minister of the second Monarchy Government (July 1976), carried out with determination and skill–helped by a broad social consensus–the so-called transition to democracy. The transition, after going through several stages (recognition of basic liberties, political parties, including the communist party, the trade unions, an amnesty for political offences, etc.), culminated in the first democratic parliamentary elections in 41 years, on June 15, 1977. The Cortes formed as a result decided to start a constituent process which concluded with the adoption of a new Constitution, ratified by universal suffrage, on December 6, 1978.

Between 1980 and 1982, the regions of Catalonia, the Basque Country, Galicia, and Andalusia approved statutes for their own self-government and elected their respective parliaments. In January 1981, the prime minister, Adolfo Suarez, resigned and was succeeded by Leopoldo Calvo-Sotelo. On August 27, 1982, Calvo-Sotelo presented to the King a decree for the dissolution of Parliament and the calling of a general election to be held on October 28th. Victory of the polls went to the Spanish Socialist Worker Party (PSOE) and its secretary general, Felipe Gonzalez. Felipe Gonzalez was elected prime minister (December 2nd) after the parliamentary vote of investiture.

The subsequent general elections of 1986, 1989 and 1993 were also won by the Spanish Socialist Party and consolidated the position of the Popular Party, led by Jose Maria Aznar, as the second largest political force in the country.

Government and Politics

Parliamentary democracy was restored following the death of General Franco in 1975, who had ruled since the end of the civil war in 1939. The 1978 constitution established Spain as a parliamentary monarchy, with the Prime Minister responsible to the bicameral Cortes elected every 4 years. On February 23, 1981, rebel elements among the security forces seized the Cortes and tried to impose a military-backed government. However, the great majority of the military forces remained loyal to King Juan Carlos, who used his personal authority to put down the bloodless coup attempt.

In March 1996, Jose Maria Aznar's Popular Party (PP) won a plurality of votes. Aznar moved to decentralize powers to the regions and liberalize the economy, with a program of privatizations, labor market reform, and measures designed to increase competition in selected markets, principally telecommunications. During Aznar's first term, Spain fully integrated into European institutions, qualifying for the European Monetary Union. During this period, Spain participated, along with the United States and other NATO allies, in military operations in the former Yugoslavia. Spanish planes took part in the air war against Serbia in 1999, and Spanish armed forces and police personnel are included in the international peacekeeping forces in Bosnia and Kosovo.

Cervantes Monument, Madrid

Bullring in Seville

Grounds of the Plaza de España

Alcazar, Segovia

Triumph Arch, Barcelona

This Phrase Book contains the Spanish expressions you are most likely to need. *All the words are written in a spelling which you read like English.* Each letter or combination of letters is used for the sound it normally represents in English and it *always* stands for the same sound. Thus, "oo" is always to be read as in *too, boot, tooth, roost,* never as in *blood* or *door.*

Syllables that are accented — that is, pronounced louder than others — are written in capitals. Curved lines (‿) are used to show sounds that are pronounced together without any break, for example, "K‿YAY-ro" meaning "I want."

5

Special Points

AY   as in *may, say, play* but cut short. It may therefore sometimes sound like the *e* in *let*. Example: "TAY" meaning "tea."

O or OA   as in *go, boat, load* but cut short. It may therefore sometimes sound like the *aw* in *law*. Examples: "NO" meaning "no," "DOAN-day" meaning "where."

H   as in *house, hat, hall* but stronger. Example: "HEF-ay" meaning "chief."

RR   stands for a strongly trilled *r*-sound, like the telephone operators' "thuh-r-r-ree" for "three." This double "rr" differs from the single "r" which is made by a quick tap of the tongue against the gums back of the teeth. Example of "rr": "fay-rro-ka-RREEL" meaning "railroad." Example of "r": "kwa-REN-ta" meaning "forty."

In Spanish there is not much difference between *b* and *v*. You will notice that the word for "Saturday," "SA-ba-do," may often sound like "SA-va-do," and the word meaning "twenty," "VAYN-tay," may sound like "BAYN-tay." You will always be understood whether you pronounce the sound of *b* or *v*.

6

Regional Differences

Since Spanish is not spoken in exactly the same way in all regions where it is used, the Phrase Book always gives the most widespread pronunciation. Thus words like "SEN-tro" (spelled *centro*) meaning "center" and "PLA-sa" (spelled *plaza*) meaning "public square" are written here with the *s*-sound used in Latin America rather than the *th*-sound used in parts of Spain. Likewise, words like "a-ma-REE-yo" (spelled *amarillo*) meaning "yellow" are written with a *y*-sound rather than with the *l‿y*-sound used in parts of Spain.

How to Use This Phrase Book

The Table of Contents lists the situations covered. Try to become familiar with the contents of the Phrase Book so that you will know where to find a given section when you need it. In each section you will find a number of questions, each one so phrased that the Spanish speaker will answer Yes or No, point out the direction, give you a number, etc. If you don't get an answer you can understand, use one of the following expressions:

English	Pronunciation	Spanish Spelling
Answer Yes or No	koan-TEST-ay SEE o NO	Conteste sí o no

7

English	Pronunciation	Spanish Spelling
Point out where it is	een-DEE-kem-ay DOAN-day ess-TA	Indíqueme donde está
Write it	esk-REE-ba-lo	Escríbalo
Write the number	esk-REE-ba el NOO-may-ro	Escriba el número

You can also point to the question in Spanish and ask the Spanish speaker to point to the answer:

Point to the answer in this book	een-DEE-kem-ay la rresp-WEST-ah en EST-ay LEE-bro	Indíqueme la respuesta en este libro

The expression for "please" is "por fa-VOR":

Please point out where it is	een-DEE-kem-ay DOAN-day ess-TA, por fa-VOR	Indíqueme donde está por favor

It is a good idea to memorize the words for "Yes" and "No," the numbers (at least up to ten) and other expressions you will constantly need.

When you need only a single word, use the Alphabetical Word List at the back of the book.

Fill-in Sentences

Many of the expressions are given in the form of fill-in sentences, each containing a blank which you fill in with any of the words in the list that follows. For example, if you want to know where the station is, you can look either in the section headed Location or in the one headed Roads and Transportation. You will find an expression for "Where is ___?" and, in the list following it, the word for "station." You then combine them as follows:

Where is ___?	DOAN-day ess-TA ___?	¿Dónde está ___?
the railroad station	la est-ahss-YOAN del fay-rro-ka-RREEL	la estación del ferrocarril
Where is the railroad station?	DOAN-day est-TA la est-ahss-YOAN del fay-rro-ka-RREEL?	¿Dónde está la estación del ferrocarril?

Sometimes the blank has to be filled in with the name of a city or person. For example:

How far is —?	ah KAY dee-STAHNSS-ya ess-TA ___?	¿A qué distancia está ___?
___ wants to see you	___ K‿YAY-ray VAYR-lo ah oo-STED	___ quiere verlo a usted

EMERGENCY EXPRESSIONS

ASKING HELP

English	Pronunciation	Spanish Spelling
Help!	ow-SEEL-yo!	¡Auxilio!
Help me	ah-YOO-dem-ay	Ayúdeme
I am lost	may ay payr-DEED-o	Me he perdido
Do you understand?	koam-PREN-day oo-STED?	¿Comprende usted?
Yes	SEE	Sí
No	NO	No
I don't understand	NO koam-PREND-o	No comprendo
Speak slowly	AH-blay dess-PAHSS-yo	Hable despacio
Say it again	rray-PEE-ta-lo	Repítalo
Please	por fa-VOR	Por favor
Where is a town?	DOAN-day A_ee oon po-BLA-do?	¿Dónde hay un poblado?
Please show me	en-SEN-yem-ay	Enséñeme

English	Pronunciation	Spanish Spelling
Draw me a map	dee-BOO-hem-ay oon PLA-no	Dibújeme un plano
Where are they?	DOAN-day ess-TAHN?	¿Dónde están?
How can I get there?	KO-mo PWED-o yay-GAR ah-YEE?	¿Cómo puedo llegar allí?
Is there a train?	A‿ee TREN?	¿Hay tren?
Where is the station?	DOAN-day ess-TA la est-ahss-YOAN?	¿Dónde está la estación?
Is there a bus?	A‿ee out-o-BOOSS?	¿Hay autobús?
Where can I get the bus?	DOAN-day PWED-o to-MAR el out-o-BOOSS?	¿Dónde puedo tomar el autobús?

Royal Palace, Madrid

English	Pronunciation	Spanish Spelling
Take me there	YEV-em-ay ah-YA	Lléveme allá
You will be rewarded	say lay gra-tee-fee-ka-RA	Se le gratificará
I want to eat	K~YAY-ro ko-MAYR	Quiero comer
I want water	K~YAY-ro AH-gwa	Quiero agua
Where can I get food?	DOAN-day PWED-o koan-say-GEER ko-MEE-da?	¿Dónde puedo conseguir comida?
I am wounded	ess-TOY ay-REE-do	Estoy herido

NOTE: See Medical Aid, pages 33-36.

Take me to a doctor	YEV-em-ay ah oon MED-ee-ko	Lléveme a un médico
Bring a doctor	TRA~ee-ga oon MED-ee-ko	Traiga un médico
Bring help!	TRA~ee-ga ah-YOO-da!	¡Traiga ayuda!

WARNINGS

Danger!	pay-LEE-gro!	¡Peligro!
Don't smoke!	NO foo-MAR!	¡No fumar!
Careful!	kwee-DA-do!	¡Cuidado!
Look out!	TEN-ga kwee-DA-do!	¡Tenga cuidado!

12

English	Pronunciation	Spanish Spelling
Lie down!	ah-KWEST-ess-ay!	¡Acuéstese!
Get down!	ah-GA-chess-ay!	¡Agáchese!
Quiet!	see-LENSS-yo!	¡Silencio!
Take cover!	POAN-ga-say ah koob-YAYRT-o!	¡Póngase a cubierto!

Alcazar, Toledo

13

Segovia's Roman aqueduct

GENERAL EXPRESSIONS

GREETINGS

English	Pronunciation	Spanish Spelling
Hello!	O-la!	¡Hola!
Good morning *or* Good day	BWEN-oas DEE-ahss	Buenos días
Good afternoon	BWEN-ahss TAR-dess	Buenas tardes
Good evening *or* Good night	BWEN-ahss NO-chess	Buenas noches
How are you?	KO-mo ess-TA oo-STED?	¿Cómo está usted?
I am well	ess-TOY B⌣YEN	Estoy bien
Thank you	GRAHSS-yahss	Gracias
You're welcome	NO A⌣ee day KAY	No hay de qué
Please	por fa-VOR	Por favor
Pardon me	dee-SPEN-sem-ay	Dispénseme
Sir *or* Mr.	sen-YOR	Señor
Madam *or* Mrs.	sen-YO-ra	Señora
Miss	sen-yo-REE-ta	Señorita
My name is __	may YA-mo __	Me llamo __

English	Pronunciation	Spanish Spelling
What is your name?	KO-mo say YA-ma oo-STED?	¿Cómo se llama usted?
Glad to meet you	MOO-cho GOO-sto en ko-no-SAYR-lay	Mucho gusto en conocerle
Come in	EN-tray	Entre
Sit down	S‿YEN-tess-ay	Siéntese
here	ah-KEE	aquí
there	ah-YEE	allí
Make yourself comfortable	POAN-ga-say ah sooss AHN-chahss	Póngase a sus anchas
Have a cigarette	TO-may oon see-ga-RREE-yo	Tome un cigarrillo
Do you have a light?	T‿YEN-ay oo-STED kahn-DEL-ah?	¿Tiene usted candela?
Are you hungry?	T‿YEN-ay oo-STED AHM-bray?	¿Tiene usted hambre?
Are you thirsty?	T‿YEN-ay oo-STED SED?	¿Tiene usted sed?
Good-by	ahd-YOASS	Adiós
See you again	AH-sta la VEE-sta	Hasta la vista
See you later	AH-sta LWEG-o	Hasta luego
See you tomorrow	AH-sta mahn-YA-na	Hasta mañana
See you soon	AH-sta PROANT-o	Hasta pronto
Good luck	BWEN-ah SWAYR-tay	Buena suerte

16

PHRASES TO HELP UNDERSTANDING

Yes	SEE	Sí
No	NO	No
Maybe	kee-SAHSS	Quizás
Certainly	say-GOO-ro	Seguro
Doubtless	seen DOO-da	Sin duda
I don't know	NO SAY	No sé
I think so	KRAY-o kay SEE	Creo que sí
I don't think so	KRAY-o kay NO	Creo que no
What languages do you speak?	KAY eed-YO-mahss AH-bla oo-STED?	¿Qué idiomas habla usted?
Do you speak ___?	AH-bla oo-STED ___?	¿Habla usted ___?
Arabic	AH-ray-bay	árabe
French	frahn-SESS	francés
German	ah-lay-MAHN	alemán
Italian	ee-tahl-YA-no	italiano
Portuguese	por-too-GESS	portugués
Brazilian	bra-see-LEN-yo	brasileño
I speak ___	AH-blo ___	Hablo ___
I don't speak well	NO AH-blo B⌐YEN	No hablo bien
Can you get an interpreter?	PWED-ay oo-STED ah-YAR oon een-TAYR-pret-ay?	¿Puede usted hallar un intérprete?

English	Pronunciation	Spanish Spelling
I don't understand	NO koam-PREND-o	No comprendo
Speak slowly	AH-blay dess-PAHSS-yo	Hable despacio
Do you understand?	koam-PREN-day oo-STED?	¿Comprende usted?
What?	KAY?	¿Qué?
Repeat	rray-PEE-ra-lo	Repítalo
What do you call this?	KO-mo say YA-ma EST-o?	¿Cómo se llama esto?
What is this?	KAY ess EST-o?	¿Qué es esto?
What is that?	KAY ess ESS-o?	¿Qué es eso?
Wait a moment	ess-PAY-ray oon mo-MENT-o	Espere un momento
Come with me	VEN-ga koan-MEE-go	Venga conmigo
__ wants to see you	__ K‿YAY-ray VAYR-lo ah oo-STED	__ quiere verlo a usted
I want to ask you some questions	K‿YAY-ro ah-SAYR-lay al-GOO-nahss pray-GOON-tahss	Quiero hacerle algunas preguntas
Answer Yes or No	koan-TEST-ay SEE o NO	Conteste sí o no
Point out where it is	een-DEE-kem-ay DOAN-day ess-TA	Indíqueme donde está
Write it	esk-REE-ba-lo	Escríbalo

18

English	Pronunciation	Spanish Spelling
Write the number	esk-REE-ba el NOO-may-ro	Escriba el número
Point to the answer in this book	een-DEE-kay la rresp-WEST-ah en EST-ay LEE-bro	Indique la respuesta en este libro
Draw a picture of it	dee-BOO-hay-lo	Dibújelo
Tell the truth	DEE-ga la vayr-DA	Diga la verdad
You will not be hurt	NO lay pa-sa-RA NA-da	No le pasará nada
You will be rewarded	say lay gra-tee-fee-ka-RA	Se le gratificará

QUESTIONS ABOUT AN INDIVIDUAL

What nationality are you?	KWAHŁ ess soo nahss-yo-na-lee-DA?	¿Cuál es su nacionalidad?
Are you ___?	ESS oo-STED ___?	¿Es usted ___?
French	frahn-SESS	francés
Greek	gree-EG-o	griego
Italian	ee-tahl-YA-no	italiano.
Portuguese	por-too-GESS	portugués
Spanish	esp-ahn-YOAL	español
Mexican	may-hee-KA-no	mexicano
Central American	sen-tro-ah-may-ree-KA-no	centroamericano
South American	soo-da-may-ree-KA-no	sudamericano

English	Pronunciation	Spanish Spelling
Are you from this region?	ess oo-STED day EST-ah rrehh-YOAN?	¿Es usted de esta región?
Where are you from?	day DOAN-day ess oo-STED?	¿De dónde es usted?
I am from ___	soy day ___	Soy de ___
Where do you live?	DOAN-day VEE-vay oo-STED?	¿Dónde vive usted?
I live in ___	VEE-vo en ___	Vivo en ___
Where are you going?	ah DOAN-day VA oo-STED?	¿A dónde va usted?
I am going to ___	VOY ah ___	Voy a ___
Where are your friends?	DOAN-day ess-TAHN sooss ah-MEE-goass?	¿Dónde están sus amigos?
Are they ___?	ess-TAHN ___?	¿Están ___?
near	SAYR-ka	cerca
far	LAY-hoass	lejos
Show your identification	MWEST-ray la SED-oo-la day ee-den-tee-DA	Muestre la cédula de identidad
Where is your ___?	DOAN-day ess-TA soo ___?	¿Dónde está su ___?
chief	HEF-ay	jefe
family	fa-MEEL-ya	familia
father	PA-dray	padre
mother	MA-dray	madre
husband	ma-REED-o	marido
wife	ess-PO-sa	esposa

20

Cathedral, Bugos

Statue of a Moorish notable

Avila's city walls, 11th century

Cathedral, Zaragoza

Cathedral, Siguenza

Puerto del Alcazar, Avila

PERSONAL NEEDS

FOOD AND DRINK

I am hungry	TEN-go AHM-bray	Tengo hambre
I am thirsty	TEN-go SED	Tengo sed
Where is there water?	DOAN-day A‿ee AH-gwa?	¿Dónde hay agua?
Where is a restaurant?	DOAN-day A‿ee oon rrest-ow-RAHN-tay?	¿Dónde hay un restaurante?
I want to buy food	K‿YAY-ro koam-PRAR ko-MEE-da	Quiero comprar comida
Is this good to __?	say __ EST-o?	¿Se __ esto?
eat	KO-may	come
drink	BEB-ay	bebe
I want __	K‿YAY-ro __	Quiero __
Give me __	DEM-ay __	Déme __
Bring me __	TRA‿ee-ga-may __	Tráigame __
food	ko-MEE-da	comida
water	AH-gwa	agua
beans	free-HO-less	frijoles
beef	KAR-nay day VA-ka	carne de vaca

English	Pronunciation	Spanish Spelling
beets	rrem-o-LA-cha	remolacha
bread	PAHN	pan
butter	mahn-tay-KEE-ya	mantequilla
cabbage	KOAL	col
candy	DOOL-sess	dulces
cheese	KESS-o	queso
chicken	PO-yo	pollo
chocolate	cho-ko-LA-tay	chocolate
clams	ahl-MAY-hahss	almejas
eggs	WEV-oass	huevos
fish	pess-KA-do	pescado
lamb	kor-DAY-ro	cordero
lentils	len-TAY-hahss	lentejas
lettuce	lay-CHOO-ga	lechuga
lobster	lahn-GO-sta	langosta
meat	KAR-nay	carne
oysters	O-strahss	ostras
pork	SAYRD-o	cerdo
potatoes	PA-pahss	papas
rice	ah-RROASS	arroz
soup	SO-pa	sopa
spinach	esp-ee-NA-kahss	espinacas
squash	ka-la-BA-sa	calabaza
steak	beef-TEK	biftec
tomatoes	to-MA-tess	tomates
turnips	NA-boass	nabos
vegetables	lay-GOOM-bress	legumbres

English	Pronunciation	Spanish Spelling
apples	mahn-SA-nahss	manzanas
bananas	ba-NA-noass	bananos
cherries	say-RESS-ahss	cerezas
coconuts	KO-koass	cocos
dates	DA-tee-less	dátiles
lemons	lee-MO-ness	limones
grapes	OO-vahss	uvas
mangoes	MAHN-goass	mangos
oranges	na-RAHN-hahss	naranjas
peaches	mel-o-ko-TOAN-ess	melocotones
pears	PAY-rahss	peras
pineapples	PEEN-yahss	piñas
plums	seer-WEL-ahss	ciruelas
strawberries	FRESS-ahss	fresas
watermelon	sahn-DEE-ah	sandía
beer	sayr-VESS-ah	cerveza
boiled water	AH-gwa ayr-VEE-da	agua hervida
brandy	BRAHN-dee	brandy
coffee	ka-FAY	café
coffee with milk	ka-FAY koan LECH-ay	café con leche
cream	KREM-ah	crema
drinking water	AH-gwa po-TA-blay	agua potable

English	Pronunciation	Spanish Spelling
milk	LECH-ay	leche
tea	TAY	té
wine	VEE-no	vino
pepper	peem-YEN-ta	pimienta
salt	SAHL	sal
sugar	ah-SOO-kar	azúcar
vinegar	vee-NA-gray	vinagre
a cup	oo-na TA-sa	una taza
a fork	oon ten-ay-DOR	un tenedor
a glass	oon VA-so	un vaso
a knife	oon koo-CHEE-yo	un cuchillo
a plate	oon PLA-to	un plato
a spoon	oo-na koo-CHA-ra	una cuchara
I want it ___	lo K˅YAY-ro ___	Lo quiero ___
cooked	ko-see-NA-do	cocinado
raw	KROOD-o	crudo
rare	PO-ko ah-SA-do	poco asado
well done	B˅YEN ko-SEED-o	bien cocido
baked	ECH-o ahl OR-no	hecho al horno
boiled	ko-SEED-o	cocido
broiled *or* roasted	ah-SA-do	asado
fried	FREET-o	frito
Give my horse ___	DEL-ay ___ ah mee ka-BA-yo	Déle ___ a mi caballo
feed	day ko-MAYR	de comer
water	AH-gwa	agua

30

LODGING

Where is a hotel?	DOAN-day A_ee oon o-TEL?	¿Dónde hay un hotel?
I want to spend the night	K_YAY-ro pa-SAR la NO-chay	Quiero pasar la noche
I want___	K_YAY-ro ___	Quiero ___
a bed	oo-na KA-ma	una cama
bedding	RRO-pa day KA-ma	ropa de cama
blankets	fra-SA-dahss	frazadas
hot water	AH-gwa kahl-YEN-tay	agua caliente
insecticide	een-sek-tee-SEE-da	insecticida
a light	oo-na LOOSS	una luz
mosquito netting	oon mo-skee-TAY-ro	un mosquitero
a pillow	oo-na ahl-mo-AH-da	una almohada
a room	oon KWART-o	un cuarto
soap	ha-BOAN	jabón
toilet paper	pa-PEL eeh-YEN-ee-ko	papel higiénico
a towel	oo-na to-AH-ya	una toalla
Where is the toilet?	DOAN-day ees-TA el esk-oo-SA-do?	¿Dónde está el excusado?
I want ___	K_YAY-ro ___	Quiero ___
to sleep	dor-MEER	dormir
to wash	la-VAR-may	lavarme
to bathe	bahn-YAR-may	bañarme
the key	la YA-vay	la llave

31

English	Pronunciation	Spanish Spelling
Call me at ___	YA-mem-ay ah lahss	Llámeme a las ___

NOTE: See Numbers, page 57, and Time, pages 70-71.

Have you any messages for me?	A͟ee rray-KA-doass pa-ra MEE?	¿Hay recados para mí?
Give this message to ___	DEL-ay EST-ay rray-KA-do ah ___	Déle este recado a ___
Here is my address	ah-KEE T͟YEN-ay mee dee-reks-YOAN	Aquí tiene mi dirección
Forward mail	rreks-PEE-da-say la ko-rresp-oan-DENSS-ya	Reexpídase la correspondencia
Send my things	MAHN-day meess KO-sahss	Mande mis cosas
I shall return ___	voal-vay-RAY ___	Volveré ___
tomorrow	mahn-YA-na	mañana
Wednesday	el M͟YAYR-ko-less	el miércoles
Have you a ___ room?	T͟YEN-ay oo-STED oon KWART-o ___?	¿Tiene usted un cuarto ___?
better	may-HOR	mejor
larger	ma-YOR	mayor
cheaper	mahs ba-RA to	más barato

32

MEDICAL AID

English	Pronunciation	Spanish
Help!	ow-SEEL-yo!	¡Auxilio!
Where is ___?	DOAN-day A‿ee ___?	¿Dónde hay ___?
Call ___	YA-may ah ___	Llame a ___
a doctor	oon MED-ee-ko	un médico
a dentist	oon den-TEE-sta	un dentista
an ambulance	oo-na ahm-boo-LAHNSS-ya	una ambulancia
a nurse	oo-na en-fayr-MAY-ra	una enfermera
Quick!	PROANT-o!	¡Pronto!
Stop the bleeding!	PA-ray la SAHN-gray!	¡Pare la sangre!
A tourniquet!	oon tor-nee-KET-ay!	¡Un torniquete!
Tie it here	AH-tel-o ah-KEE	Atelo aquí
Above the wound	MAHSS ah-RREE-ba de la ay-REE-da	Más arriba de la herida
I am ___	ess-TOY ___	Estoy ___
He is ___	ess-TA ___	Está ___
sick	en-FAYR-mo	enfermo
wounded	ay-REE-do	herido

English	Pronunciation	Spanish Spelling
My ___ hurts	may DWEL-ay ___	Me duele ___
head	la ka-BESS-ah	la cabeza
tooth	la MWEL-ah	la muela
back	la ess-PAHL-da	la espalda
stomach	el ess-TOAM-ah-go	el estómago
I am hurt here	may ay ECH-o DAHN-yo ah-KEE	Me he hecho daño aquí
I am hurt in ___	may ay ECH-o DAHN-yo en ___	Me he hecho daño en ___
He is hurt in ___	say ah ECH-o DAHN-yo en ___	Se ha hecho daño en ___
the head	la ka-BESS-ah	la cabeza
the face	la KA-ra	la cara
the eye	el O-ho	el ojo
the inner ear	el o-EE-do	el oído
the outer ear	la o-RAY-ha	la oreja
the nose	la na-REESS	la nariz
the mouth	la BO-ka	la boca
the jaw	la kee-HA-da	la quijada
the throat	la gar-GAHN-ta	la garganta
the neck	el KWAY-yo	el cuello
the shoulder	el OAM-bro	el hombro
the arm	el BRA-so	el brazo
the elbow	el KOAD-o	el codo

34

English	Pronunciation	Spanish Spelling
the hand	la MA-no	la mano
the back	la ess-PAHL-da	la espalda
the chest	el PECH-o	el pecho
the stomach	el ess-TOAM-ah-go	el estómago
the hip	la ka-DAY-ra	la cadera
the groin	la EEN-glay	la ingle
the privates	lahss PAR-tess	las partes
the leg	la P_YAYR-na	la pierna
the knee	la rro-DEE-ya	la rodilla
the ankle	el to-BEE-yo	el tobillo
the foot	el P_YAY	el pie
Bring ——	TRA_ee-ga ——	Traiga ——
a blanket	oo-na fra-SA-da	una frazada
blankets	fra-SA-dahss	frazadas
boiled water	AH-gwa ayr-VEE-da	agua hervida
cotton	ahl-go-DOAN	algodón
a disinfectant	oon dess-een-fek-TAHN-tay	un desinfectante
drinking water	AH-gwa po-TA-blay	agua potable
hot water	AH-gwa kahl-YEN-tay	agua caliente
ice	YEL-o	hielo
a knife	oon koo-CHEE-yo	un cuchillo

English	Pronunciation	Spanish Spelling
a sedative	oon sed-ah-TEE-vo	un sedativo
sheets	SA-ba-nahss	sábanas
something to bandage with	AHL-go pa-ra ven-DAR	algo para vendar
splints	ta-BLEE-yahss	tablillas
a stimulant	oon est-ee-moo-LAHN-tay	un estimulante
Be careful	TEN-ga kwee-DA-do	Tenga cuidado
Do not touch ___	NO ___ TOAK-ay	No ___ toque
Do not move ___	NO ___ MWEV-ah	No ___ mueva
Lift ___ carefully	lay-VAHN-tay ___ koan kwee-DA-do	Levánte ___ con cuidado
me	may	me
him	lo	lo
them	loass	los
Do not give him that	NO lay DAY ESS-o	No le dé eso
I have been poisoned	may ay en-ven-ay-NA-do	Me he envenenado
He has been poisoned	say ah en-ven-ay-NA-do	Se ha envenenado
by water	koan AH-gwa	con agua
by food	koan ah-lee-MENT-o	con alimento
by gas	koan GAHSS	con gas
by a snakebite	koan pee-ka-DOO-ra day koo-LEB-ra	con picadura de culebra

BUYING AND PERSONAL SERVICES

Where To Get It

Where is ___?	DOAN-day A_ee ___?	¿Dónde hay ___?
a barber	oon bar-BAY-ro	un barbero
a bathhouse	oo-na KA-sa day BAHN-yoass	una casa de baños
a drug store	oo-na bo-TEE-ka	una botica
a grocery	oo-na bo-DEG-ah	una bodega
a movie	oon SEE-nay	un cine
a restaurant	oon rrest-ow-RAHN-tay	un restaurante
a tailor	oon SA-stray	un sastre

Things Wanted

I want to buy ___	K_YAY-ro koam-PRAR ___	Quiero comprar ___
Where can I get ___?	DOAN-day PWED-o koan-say-GEER ___?	¿Dónde puedo conseguir ___?
I want ___	K_YAY-ro	Quiero ___
Give me ___	DEM-ay ___	Déme ___
this	EST-o	esto
that	ESS-o	eso
one of these	oo-no day EST-oass	uno de estos

English	Pronunciation	Spanish Spelling
alcohol	ahl-KOAL	alcohol
ammonia	ah-moan-YA-ko	amoníaco
aspirin	ah-spee-REE-na	aspirina
a bandage	oo-na VEN-da	una venda
batteries	ba-tay-REE-ahss	baterías
bay rum	ahl-ko-LA-do	alcoholado
a belt	oon seen-too-ROAN	un cinturón
a brush	oon say-PEE-yo	un cepillo
buttons	bo-TOAN-ess	botones
cigarettes	see-ga-RREE-yoass	cigarrillos
cloth	TEL-ah	tela
a coat	oo-na cha-KET-ah	una chaqueta
a comb	oon PAY‿ee-nay	un peine
cotton	ahl-go-DOAN	algodón
a disinfectant	oon dess-een-fek-TAHN-tay	un desinfectante
envelopes	SO-bress	sobres
a flashlight	oo-na leen-TAYR-na ay-LEK-tree-ka	una linterna eléctrica
foot powder	POAL-voass pa-ra loass P‿YESS	polvos para los pies
gloves	GWAHN-tess	guantes
goggles	ahn-tay-O-hoass day ka-MEE-no	anteojos de camino
handkerchiefs	pahn-yoo-EL-oass	pañuelos
a hat	oon soam-BRAY-ro	un sombrero

English	Pronunciation	Spanish Spelling
ink	TEEN-ta	tinta
iodine	YO-do	yodo
a knife	oon koo-CHEE-yo	un cuchillo
a laxative	oon lahk-SAHN-tay	un laxante
a light bulb	oo-na boam-BEE-ya	una bombilla
matches	FO-sfo-roass	fósforos
a needle	oo-na ah-GOO-ha	una aguja
an overcoat	oon so-bray-TOAD-o	un sobretodo
pants	pahn-ta-LO-ness	pantalones
paper	pa-PEL	papel
a pencil	oon LA-peess	un lápiz
pins	ahl-fee-LAY-ress	alfileres
quinine	kee-NEE-na	quinina
a raincoat	oon eem-payr-may-AH-blay	un impermeable
a razor	oo-na na-VA-ha day ah-fay-TAR	una navaja de afeitar
razor blades	O-hahss day ah-fay-TAR	hojas de afeitar
rubbing alcohol	ahl-KOAL day fro-TAR	alcohol de frotar
a scarf	oo-na boo-FAHN-da	una bufanda
scissors	tee-HAY-rahss	tijeras
shaving cream	KREM-ah day ah-fay-TAR	crema de afeitar

39

English	Pronunciation	Spanish Spelling
a shirt	oo-na ka-MEE-sa	una camisa
shoelaces	kor-DOAN-ess day sa-PA-toass	cordones de zapatos
shoes	sa-PA-toass	zapatos
soap	ha-BOAN	jabón
socks	kahl-say-TEE-ness	calcetines
sunglasses	GA-fahss ow-MA-dahss	gafas ahumadas
a sweater	oon SWET-ayr	un sweater
thread	EE-lo	hilo
a toothbrush	oon say-PEE-yo day D‿YEN-tess	un cepillo de dientes
toothpaste	PA-sta den-TEE-free-ka	pasta dentífrica
tooth powder	POAL-voass den-TEE-free-koass	polvos dentífricos
underwear	RRO-pa een-tayr-YOR	ropa interior
Have you something else?	T‿YEN-ay oo-STED O-tra KO-sa?	¿Tiene usted otra cosa?
More	MAHSS	más

Services Wanted

English	Pronunciation	Spanish Spelling
I want this ___	K‿YAY-ro kay may ___ EST-o	Quiero que me ___ esto
washed	LA-ven	laven
pressed	PLAHN-chen	planchen
dry cleaned	LEEMP-yen	limpien
repaired	koam-POAN-gahn	compongan

English	Pronunciation	Spanish Spelling
Where can I get some clothes ___?	DOAN-day PWED-o mahn-DAR ah ___ RRO-pa?	¿Dónde puedo mandar a ___ ropa?
washed	la-VAR	lavar
pressed	plahn-CHAR	planchar
dry cleaned	leemp-YAR	limpiar
mended	rrem-en-DAR	remendar
I want to hire ___	K⌣YAY-ro ahl-kee-LAR ___	Quiero alquilar ___
I want to borrow ___	K⌣YAY-ro pay-DEER press-TA-do ___	Quiero pedir prestado ___
this	EST-o	esto
that	ESS-o	eso
I want ___	K⌣YAY-ro ___	Quiero ___
a haircut	kor-TAR-may el PEL-o	cortarme el pelo
a shave	ah-fay-TAR-may	afeitarme
a guide	oon GHEE-ah	un guía
a porter	oon MO-so	un mozo
a taxi	oon TAHK-see	un taxi
a driver	oon cho-FAYR	un chofer
someone to help me	AHLG-yen kay may ah-YOO-day	alguien que me ayude

41

Payment

NOTE: See Numbers, page 57.

English	Pronunciation	Spanish Spelling
How much?	KWAHNT-o?	¿Cuánto?
How much is ___?	KWAHNT-o ess ___?	¿Cuánto es ___?
I will pay you	lay pa-ga-RAY	Le pagaré
This is American money	EST-ay ess dee-NAY-ro nor-tay-ah-may-ree-KA-no	Este es dinero norte-americano
It is worth ___	VA-lay ___	Vale ___
Not so much	NO TAHNT-o	No tanto
That is too much	ESS-o ess dem-ahss-YA-do	Eso es demasiado
I will pay ___	pa-ga-RAY ___	Pagaré ___
No more	NO MAHSS	No más
Will you sell this for ___?	may VEN-day oo-STED EST-o por ___?	¿Me vende usted esto por ___?
You owe me ___	oo-STED may DEB-ay ___	Usted me debe ___
I want a receipt	K⌣YAY-ro oon rray-SEE-bo	Quiero un recibo
Here is a receipt	ah-KEE T⌣YEN-ay oon rray-SEE-bo	Aquí tiene un recibo
Take it to this address	YEV-el-o ah EST-ah dee-reks-YOAN	Llévelo a esta dirección
You will be paid on delivery	say lay pa-ga-RA ahl en-tray-GAR	Se le pagará al entregar

LOCATION AND TERRAIN

LOCATION

English	Pronunciation	Spanish Spelling
What place is this?	KAY loo-GAR ess EST-ay?	¿Qué lugar es éste?
Show me on this map	MWEST-ray-mel-o en EST-ay MA-pa	Muéstremelo en este mapa
Have you a map?	T‿YEN-ay oo-STED oon MA-pa ?	¿Tiene usted un mapa?
Can you draw me a map?	PWED-ay oo-STED dee-boo-HAR-may oon KRO-keess?	¿Puede usted dibujarme un croquis?
Can you guide me?	PWED-ay oo-STED G‿YAR-may?	¿Puede usted guiarme?
Can you find us a guide?	PWED-ay oo-STED koan-say-GEER-noass oon GHEE-ah?	¿Puede usted conseguir-nos un guía?

English	Pronunciation	Spanish Spelling
Where is ___?	DOAN-day ess-TA ___?	¿Dónde está ___?
the town	el PWEB-lo	el pueblo
the nearest town	el PWEB-lo mahss sayr-KA-no	el pueblo más cercano
the railroad station	la est-ahss-YOAN del fay-rro-ka-RREEL	la estación del ferrocarril
a telephone	oon tay-LEF-o-no	un teléfono
the U.S. Consulate	el koan-soo-LA-do day loass ess-TA-doass oo-NEE-doass	el consulado de los Estados Unidos
the power plant	la PLAHN-ta ay-LEK-tree-ka	la planta eléctrica
the police station	el kwar-TEL day po-lee-SEE-ah	el cuartel de policía
Is there ___ near here?	A ee ___ sayr-ka day ah-KEE?	¿Hay ___ cerca de aquí?
a river	ahl-GOON RREE-o	algún río
a well	ahl-GOON PO-so	algún pozo
a railroad	fay-rro-ka-RREEL	ferrocarril
a radio station	ahl-GOO-na est-ahss-YOAN day RRAHD-yo	alguna estación de radio
a town	ahl-GOON PWEB-lo	algún pueblo
a city	ahl-GOO-na s yoo-DA	alguna ciudad

English	Pronunciation	Spanish Spelling
What is its name?	KO-mo say YA-ma?	¿Cómo se llama?
What others are there?	KAY O-troass A͟ee?	¿Qué otros hay?
Point out where it is	een-DEE-kem-ay DOAN•day ess-TA	Indíqueme dónde está
Thank you	GRAHSS-yahss	Gracias
Show me	MWEST-rem-ay	Muéstreme
Which way is north?	DOAN-day KED-ah el NOR-tay?	¿Dónde queda el norte?
This way	por ah-KEE	Por aquí
That way	por ah-YEE	Por allí
To the ___	ahss-ya ___	Hacia ___
left	la eesk-YAYR-da	la izquierda
right	la day-RECH-ah	la derecha
north	el NOR-tay	el norte
northeast	el no-REST-ay	el noreste
east	el EST-ay	el este
southeast	el sood-EST-ay	el sudeste
south	el SOOR	el sur
southwest	el sood-o-EST-ay	el sudoeste
west	el o-EST-ay	el oeste
northwest	el nor-o-EST-ay	el noroeste
Here	ah-KEE	Aquí
There	ah-YEE	Allí

45

DISTANCE

How far is ___?	ah KAY dee-STAHNSS-ya ess-TA ___?	¿A qué distancia está ___?
Is it ___?	ess-TA ___?	¿Está ___?
far	LAY-hoass	lejos
very far	MOO‿ee LAY-hoass	muy lejos
near	SAYR-ka	cerca
One kilometer	oon kee-LO-met-ro	Un kilómetro
___ kilometers	___ kee-LO-met-roass	___ kilómetros
___ meters	___ MET-roass	___ metros

NOTE: See Numbers, page 57.

How many kilometers from here?	AH KWAHNT-oass kee-LO-met-roass day ah-KEE?	¿A cuántos kilómetros de aquí?

NOTE: A kilometer is about 5⁄8 of a mile. A meter is about 39 inches.

NATURE OF TERRAIN

Are you familiar with this region?	ko-NO-say oo-STED EST-ay tay-rree-TOR-yo?	¿Conoce usted este territorio?

English	Pronunciation	Spanish Spelling
Is it __?	ESS __?	¿Es __?
rocky	rro-KO-so	rocoso
flat	YA-no	llano
dry	SEK-o	seco
wet	OO-med-o	húmedo
impassable	een-trahn-see-TA-blay	intransitable
muddy	fahn-GO-so	fangoso
Are there —?	A_ee __?	¿Hay __?
glaciers	ay-LAY-roass	heleros
hills	SAY-rroass	cerros
jungles	SEL-vahss	selvas
lakes	LA-goass	lagos
mountains	moan-TAHN-yahss	montañas
passes	PA-soass	pasos
paths	vay-RED-ahss	veredas
rivers	RREE-oass	ríos
roads	ka-MEE-noass	caminos
springs	ma-nahnt-YA-less	manantiales
woods	BO-skess	bosques
Is the water deep?	ess pro-FOON-da el AH-gwa?	¿Es profunda el agua?
Are the mountains high?	soan AHL-tahss lahss moan-TAHN-yahss?	¿Son altas las montañas?
Is the current swift?	ess RRA-pee-da la korr-YEN-tay?	¿Es rápida la corriente?
Is there a bridge?	A_ee PWEN-tay?	¿Hay puente?

47

ROADS AND TRANSPORTATION

ROADS AND BRIDGES

English	Pronunciation	Spanish Spelling
What town does this road lead to?	ah KAY PWEB-lo VA EST-ay ka-MEE-no?	¿A qué pueblo va este camino?
Is the road ___?	ess ___ el ka-MEE-no?	¿Es ___ el camino?
Is this bridge ___?	ess ___ el PWEN-tay?	¿Es ___ el puente?
good	BWEN-o	bueno
bad	MA-lo	malo
passable	pa-SA-blay	pasable
impassable	eem-pa-SA-blay	impasable
Will the bridge carry this load?	PWED-ay el PWEN-tay so-por-TAR EST-ay PESS-o?	¿Puede el puente soportar este peso?
Are there ___?	A͟ee ___?	¿Hay ___?
bridges	PWEN-tess	puentes
detours	des-VEE-òass	desvíos

English	Pronunciation	Spanish Spelling
fords	VA-doass	vados
guideposts	PO-stess een-dee-ka-DOR-ess	postes indicadores
guides	GHEE-ahss	guías
mud puddles	CHAR-koass	charcos
obstructions	oab-strooks-YO-ness	obstrucciones
narrow stretches	TRECH-oass ahn-GO-stoass	trechos angostos
potholes	BA-chess	baches
ruts	rro-DA-dahss	rodadas
snowdrifts	ven-tee-SKAY-roass	ventisqueros
What is the speed limit?	KWAHL ess la vel-o-see-DA per-mee-TEE-da?	¿Cuál es la velocidad permitida?
How fast is it safe to go?	ah KAY vel-o-see-DA say PWED-ay EER seen pay-LEE-gro?	¿A qué velocidad se puede ir sin peligro?
Do you know the road?	ko-NO-say oo-STED el ka-MEE-no?	¿Conoce usted el camino?
Please guide us	AH-ga el fa-VOR day G‿YAR-noass	Haga el favor de guiarnos
We will pay you	lay pa-ga-REM-oass	Le pagaremos
Where can we cross the river?	por DOAN-day po-DEM-oass kroo-SAR el RREE-o?	¿Por dónde podemos cruzar el río?

49

English	Pronunciation	Spanish Spelling
How deep is the river?	KAY pro-foon-dee-DA T̠YEN-ay el RREE-o?	¿Qué profundidad tiene el río?
Is the bottom __?	ESS __ el FOAND-o?	¿Es __ el fondo?
muddy	fahn-GO-so	fangoso
rocky	ped-ray-GO-so	pedregoso
sandy	ah-ray-NO-so	arenoso

RAILROADS, BUSES, PLANES

English	Pronunciation	Spanish Spelling
Where is __?	DOAN-day ess-TA __?	¿Dónde está __?
the airport	el ah̠ay-ro-PWAYR-to	el aeropuerto
the bus station	la est-ahss-YOAN del out-o-BOOSS	la estación del autobús
the railroad station	la est-ahss-YOAN del fay-rro-ka-RREEL	la estación del ferrocarril
the baggage room	la SA-la day ek-ee-PA-hess	la sala de equipajes
the ticket office	la ta-KEE-ya	la taquilla
I want to go to __	K̠YAY-ro EER ah __	Quiero ir a __
When does a __ leave?	KWAHND-o SA-lay oon __?	¿Cuándo sale un __?
bus	out-o-BOOSS	autobús
plane	ahv-YOAN	avión
train	TREN	tren

English	Pronunciation	Spanish Spelling
When does the ___ arrive?	KWAHND-o YEG-ah el ___?	¿Cuándo llega el ___?
Is the ___ running?	seer-KOO-la el ___?	¿Circula el ___?
A ticket to ___	oon bee-YET-ay pa-ra ___	Un billete para ___
What is the fare to ___?	KWAHNT-o ess el pa-SA-hay ah ___?	¿Cuánto es el pasaje a ___?
When do we get to ___?	KWAHND-o yay-GA-moass ah ___?	¿Cuándo llegamos a ___?
Give me a time-table	DEM-ay oon ee-tee-nay-RAR-yo	Déme un itinerario

OTHER MEANS OF TRANSPORTATION

English	Pronunciation	Spanish Spelling
Where can I find ___?	DOAN-day PWED-o ah-YAR ___?	¿Dónde puedo hallar ___?
a bicycle	oo-na bee-see-KLET-ah	una bicicleta
a boat	oon BO-tay	un bote
a burro	oon BOO-rro	un burro
a camel	oon ka-MAY-yo	un camello
a car	oon OUT-o	un auto
a horse	oon ka-BA-yo	un caballo
a mule	oon MOO-lo	un mulo
a plane	oon ahv-YOAN	un avión
a sleigh	oon tree-NAY-o	un trineo
a wagon	oon KA-rro	un carro

REPAIRS AND SUPPLIES

Where can I find ___?	DOAN-day PWED-o ah-YAR ___?	¿Dónde puedo hallar ___?
a battery	oon ah-koo-moo-la-DOR	un acumulador
brake fluid	LEE-kee-do pa-ra FREN-oass	líquido para frenos
a cable	oon KA-blay	un cable
chains	ka-DEN-ahss	cadenas
Diesel oil	ah-SAYT-ay D_YESS-el	aceite Diesel
distilled water	AH-gwa dest-ee-LA-da	agua destilada
an electric bulb	oo-na boam-BEE-ya	una bombilla
an electrician	oon el-ek-tree-SEE-sta	un electricista
a filling station	oon soor-tee-DOR day ga-so-LEE-na	un surtidor de gasolina
a garage	oon ga-RA-hay	un garaje
gasoline	ga-so-LEE-na	gasolina
grease	GRA-sa	grasa
an inner tube	oo-na KA-ma-ra day ba-LOAN	una cámara de balón

NOTE: In some regions, "TOO-bo een-tayr-YOR" is used instead of "KA-ma-ra." If one expression is not understood, try the other.

English	Pronunciation	Spanish Spelling
a jack	oon GA-to	un gato
a mechanic	oon may-KA-nee-ko	un mecánico
oil	ah-SAYT-ay	aceite
pliers	ah-lee-KA-tess	alicates
a screwdriver	oon dest-or-nee-ya-DOR	un destornillador
spark plugs	boo-HEE-ahss	bujías
a tire	oon nay-oo-MA-tee-ko	un neumático
tire patches	PAR-chess day nay-oo-MA-tee-ko	parches de neumático
a tire pump	BOAM-ba	bomba
tire tools	ay-rrahm-YEN-tahss	herramientas
a wrench	YA-vay een-GLESS-ah	llave inglesa

53

COMMUNICATIONS

NOTE: See Numbers, page 57.

English	Pronunciation	Spanish Spelling
__ this is __	__ day __	__ de __
Calling __	YA-mo ah __	Llamo a __
This is __	AH-bla __	Habla __
__ answers	__ koan-TEST-ah	__ contesta
__ messages for you	rray-SEE-ba __ dess-PA-choass	Reciba __ despachos
I also have messages for you	PEED-o ahl-tayr-nahss-YOAN	Pido alternación
Wait	ess-PAY-ray	Espere
Correction *or* Wrong (There is a mistake)	A⌐ee ay-RROR	Hay error

English	*Pronunciation*	*Spanish Spelling*
Read back	PEED-o ko-lahss-YOAN	Pido colación
Acknowledge	ah-KOO-say rress-eps-YOAN	Acuse recepción
Say again	rray-PEE-ta	Repita

54

English	Pronunciation	Spanish Spelling
Is this correct?	pray-GOONT-o ess ek-SAHK-to?	¿Pregunto es exacto?
That is correct	ess ek-SAHK-to	Es exacto
Speak slower	AH-blay LENT-o	Hable lento
Out (Finished)	tayr-mee-NA-do	Terminado
Urgent	oor-HEN-tay	Urgente
Do not answer	no koan-TEST-ay	No conteste

Aqueduct close-up, Segovia

TELEPHONE

Answering telephone by user	AH-bla ___	Habla ___
Number please?	NOO-may-ro?	¿Número?
Repeat	rray-PEE-ta	Repita
What number is calling?	K_YEN YA-ma?	¿Quién llama?
Hang up your receiver	en-GAHN-chay	Enganche
The line is busy	o-koo-PA-do	Ocupado
Information	een-for-mahss-YOAN	Información
Supervisor	DEM-ay ahl HEF-ay	Déme al jefe
___ does not answer	___ no koan-TEST-ah	___ no contesta
I will give you the chief operator	lay ko-moo-nee-ka-RAY koan el HEF-ay	Le comunicaré con el jefe
Here's your party	ess-TA oo-STED en ko-moo-nee-kahss-YOAN	Está usted en comunicación
___ is on the line	lay DOY ___	Le doy ___
Are you through?	tayr-mee-NA-do?	¿Terminado?
I have been disconnected	may ahn kor-TA-do	Me han cortado

56

English	Pronunciation	Spanish Spelling
I will ring again	ya-ma-RAY O-tra VESS	Llamaré otra vez
I have a call for you	AH-bla la sen-TRAHL, TEN-go oo-na ya-MA-da pa-ra oo-STED	Habla la central, tengo una llamada para usted
I must interrupt, urgent call from ___	KORT-o por OR-den day ___	Corto por orden de ___

Numbers

Numbers	Pronunciation	Numbers	Pronunciation
1	OO-no	17	d‿yess-ee-S‿YET-ay
2	DOASS	18	d‿yess-ee-O-cho
3	TRESS	19	d‿yess-ee-NWEV-ay
4	KWA-tro	20	VAYN-tay
5	SEEN-ko	21	vayn-tee-OO-no
6	SAYSS	22	vayn-tee-DOASS
7	S‿YET-ay	30	TRAYN-ta
8	O-cho	40	kwa-REN-ta
9	NWEV-ay	50	seen-KWEN-ta
10	D‿YESS	60	say-SEN-ta
11	OAN-say	70	say-TEN-ta
12	DOASS-ay	80	o-CHEN-ta
13	TRESS-ay	90	no-VEN-ta
14	ka-TOR-say	100	S‿YEN
15	KEEN-say	1,000	MEEL
16	d‿yess-ee-SAYSS		

Additional Expressions

Shall I continue to ring?	SEE-go ya-MAHN-do?	¿Sigo llamando?
I will call you back	lay ya-ma-RAY	Le llamaré
What number are you calling?	KAY NOO-may-ro day-SAY-ah oo-STED?	¿Qué número desea usted?
Give me the number of ___	DEM-ay el NOO-may-ro day ___	Déme el número de ___
Long distance	DEM-ay sayr-VEESS-yo een-tay-roor-BA-no	Déme servicio inter-urbano
Person to person	koan-fay-RENSS-ya payr-so-NAHL	Conferencia personal
Will you speak to anybody at that number?	ah-bla-REE-ah oo-STED koan kwalk-YAYR payr-SO-na kay koan-TEST-ay?	¿Hablaría usted con cualquier persona que conteste?
What is the charge?	KWAHL ess la ta-REE-fa?	¿Cuál es la tarifa?
Reverse the charges	KAR-gay-lo ahl tay-LEF-o-no kay YA-mo	Cárguelo al teléfono que llamo
Good-by	ahd-YOASS	Adiós

TELEGRAPH

I want to send a ___	day-SAY-o env-YAR oon ___	Deseo enviar un ___
telegram	tel-eg-RA-ma	telegrama

English	Pronunciation	Spanish Spelling
night letter	tel-eg-RA-ma day ma-droo-GA-da	telegrama de madrugada
day letter	tel-eg-RA-ma dee-fay-REED-o	telegrama diferido
cablegram	ka-bleg-RA-ma	cablegrama
Please give me a form	DEM-ay oon BLAHN-ko	Déme un blanco
Can I send a message to ___?	PWED-o env-YAR oon tel-eg-RA-ma ah ___?	¿Puedo enviar un telegrama a ___?
What is the charge?	KWAHL ess la ta-REE-fa?	¿Cuál es la tarifa?
Send it collect	KO-bress-ay ahl dest-ee-na-TAR-yo	Cóbrese al destinatario
Answer prepaid	koan-test-ahss-YOAN pa-GA-da	Contestación pagada

MAIL

Where is the post office?	DOAN-day ess-TA el ko-RRAY-o?	¿Dónde está el correo?
Where can I mail this?	DOAN-day PWED-o ay-CHAR ahl ko-RRAY-o EST-o?	¿Dónde puedo echar al correo esto?
How much postage on this?	KWAHNT-o frahn-KAY-o ness-ay-SEE-ta EST-o?	¿Cuánto franqueo necesita esto?

59

English	Pronunciation	Spanish Spelling
Registered	sayr-tee-fee-KA-do	Certificado
Registered with return receipt	sayr-tee-fee-KA-do koan ah-KOO-say day rray-SEE-bo	Certificado con acuse de recibo
Insured	ah-seg-oo-RA-do	Asegurado
Value ___	va-LOR ___	Valor ___
Air mail	ko-RRAY-o ah-AY-ray-o	Correo aéreo
First class	pree-MAY-ra KLA-say	Primera clase
Special delivery	en-TREG-ah een-med-YA-ta	Entrega inmediata
Parcel post	en-koam-YEN-da po-STAHL	Encomienda postal
What does it contain?	KAY koant-YEN-ay?	¿Qué contiene?
This package contains —	EST-ay pa-KET-ay koant-YEN-ay ___	Este paquete contiene ___
books	LEE-broass	libros
candy	DOOL-sess	dulces
clothing	RRO-pa	ropa
food	ko-MEE-da	comida
You may open it	PWED-ay ah-BREER-lo	Puede abrirlo
Perishable	pay-ress-ay-DAY-ro	Perecedero
Fragile	FRA-heel	Frágil
Handle with care	kwee-DA-do	Cuidado

English	Pronunciation	Spanish Spelling
Give me ___ worth of stamps	DAY-may ___ day SAY-yoass	Déme ___ de sellos

NOTE: In some regions, stamps are called "ess-tahm-PEE-yahss" and in still others "TEEM-bress."

English	Pronunciation	Spanish Spelling
Mail this	ECH-em-ay EST-o ahl ko-RRAY-o	Écheme esto al correo

La Sagrada Familia, Barcelona

Carmona, Seville

Cathedral, Seville

Palace, El Escorial

Generalife Gardens, Granada

House of Shells, Salamanca

Alhambra Walls, Granada

NUMBERS, SIZE, TIME, LETTERS, ETC.

AMOUNT

English	Pronunciation	Spanish Spelling
A few	OO-noass KWAHN-toass	unos cuantos
Several	VAR-yoass	varios
Many	MOO-choass	muchos
Not many	NO MOO-choass	no muchos
Very many	moo-CHEE-see-moass	muchísimos

ORDINAL NUMBERS

NOTE: For numbers 1-1000, see page 57.

First	pree-MAY-ro	primero
Second	say-GOOND-o	segundo
Third	tayr-SAY-ro	tercero
Fourth	KWART-o	cuarto
Fifth	KEENT-o	quinto

69

English	Pronunciation	Spanish Spelling
Sixth	SEST-o	sexto
Seventh	SEP-tee-mo	séptimo
Eighth	oak-TA-vo	octavo
Ninth	no-VEN-o	noveno
Tenth	DESS-ee-mo	décimo
Eleventh	oon-DESS-ee-mo	undécimo
Twelfth	dwo-DESS-ee-mo	duodécimo

SIZE AND WEIGHT

NOTE: For units of size and weight, see page 84.

Small	pay-KEN-yo	pequeño
Large	GRAHN-day	grande
Medium	med-YA-no	mediano
Long	LAR-go	largo
Short	KORT-o	corto
High	AHLT-o	alto
Low	BA-ho	bajo
Heavy	pay-SA-do	pesado
Light	leev-YA-no	liviano

TIME

What time is it?	KAY O-ra ess?	¿Qué hora es?
It is five o'clock	soan lahss SEEN-ko	Son las cinco

English	Pronunciation	Spanish Spelling
It is five ten	soan lahss SEEN-ko ee D⌐YESS	Son las cinco y diez
It is half past five	soan lahss SEEN-ko ee MED-ya	Son las cinco y media
It is ten to six	soan lahss SAYSS men-oas D⌐YESS	Son las seis menos diez
Today	OY	Hoy
Tomorrow	mahn-YA-na	Mañana
Yesterday	ah-YAYR	Ayer
In the __	por la __	Por la __
morning	mahn-YA-na	mañana
afternoon	TAR-day	tarde
evening	NO-chay	noche
At __	ahl __	Al __
dawn	ah-ma-nay-SAYR	amanecer
dusk	oab-skoo-ray-SAYR	obscurecer
midnight	la MED-ya NO-chay	la media noche
night	la NO-chay	la noche
noon	med-yo-DEE-ah	mediodía
Sunday	do-MEEN-go	domingo
Monday	LOO-ness	lunes
Tuesday	MAR-tess	martes
Wednesday	M⌐YAYR-ko-less	miércoles

English	Pronunciation	Spanish Spelling
Thursday	HWEV-ess	jueves
Friday	V_YAYR-ness	viernes
Saturday	SA-ba-do	sábado
January	ay-NAY-ro	enero
February	feb-RAY-ro	febrero
March	MAR-so	marzo
April	ah-BREEL	abril
May	MA-yo	mayo
June	HOON-yo	junio
July	HOOL-yo	julio
August	ah-GO-sto	agosto
September	sept-YEM-bray	septiembre
October	oak-TOO-bray	octubre
November	noav-YEM-bray	noviembre
December	deess-YEM-bray	diciembre
Week	say-MA-na	semana
Month	MESS	mes
One day	oon DEE-ah	un día
Two days	DOAS DEE-ahss	dos días
One week	OO-na say-MA-na	una semana
Two weeks	DOASS say-MA-nahss	dos semanas
One month	oon MESS	un mes
Two months	DOAS MESS-ess	dos meses

NAMES OF THE LETTERS

Letter	Pronunciation	Letter	Pronunciation
a	AH	n	EN-ay
b	BAY	ñ	EN-yay
c	SAY	o	O
ch	CHAY	p	PAY
d	DAY	q	KOO
e	AY	r	AY-rray
f	EF-ay	s	ESS-ay
g	HAY	t	TAY
h	AH-chay	u	OO
i	EE	v	VAY
j	HO-ta	w	DO-blay VAY
k	KA	x	EK-eess
l	EL-ay	y	EE gree-EG-ah
ll	AY-yay	z	SET-ah
m	EM-ay		

Convent of Las Duenas, Salamanca

Olite Castle near Pamplona

Central Palace, Seville

Myrtle's Court, Alhambra, Granada

Puerto de la Duquesa, Malaga

Alcazaba Castle, Almeria

Mosque, Cordoba

Belmonte Castle in La Mancha

Cibeles Fountain, Madrid

Plaza de España

83

Weights and Measures

The metric system of weights and measures is commonly used in many countries.

Pronunciation	Abbreviation	Spanish Spelling	English Equivalent
to-nay-LA-da MET-ree-ka	tm.	tonelada métrica	2200 pounds
keen-TAHL MET-ree-ko	qm.	quintal métrico	220 pounds
KEE-lo	kg.	kilo	2.2 pounds
GRA-mo	g.	gramo	0.035 ounce
ek-to-LEE-tro	hl.	hectolitro	26.5 gallons
LEE-tro	l.	litro	1.06 quarts
kee-LO-metro	km.	kilómetro	0.62 mile
MET-ro	m.	metro	1.1 yards or 39.37 inches
sen-TEE-met-ro	cm.	centímetro	0.39 inch
mee-LEE-met-ro	mm.	milímetro	0.039 inch

Table of Equivalents

1 tm. = 1000 kg.

1 qm. = 100 kg.

1 kg. = 1000 g.

1 hl. = 100 l.

1 km. = 1000 m.

1 m. = 100 cm.

1 m. = 1000 mm.

Table of Approximate Conversions

Inches to centimeters: Multiply by 10 and divide by 4.

Yards to meters: Multiply by 9 and divide by 10.

Miles to kilometers: Multiply by 8 and divide by 5.

Gallons to liters: Multiply by 4 and subtract 1/5 of the number of gallons.

Pounds to kilograms: Multiply by 5 and divide by 11.

IMPORTANT SIGNS

Spanish	*English*
Alto	Stop
Despacio	Go Slow
Desvío	Detour
Precaución	Caution
Peligro	Danger
Sentido único	One Way Street
No hay paso	No Thoroughfare
No hay salida	Dead End
Conserve su derecha	Keep to the Right
Viraje rápido *or* **Curva peligrosa**	Dangerous Curve
Ferrocarril	Railroad
Puente	Bridge

Spanish	*English*
Cruce	Crossroad
Cables a alta tensión	High Tension Lines
Señores *or* Hombres *or* Caballeros	Men
Señoras *or* Mujeres *or* Damas	Women
Lavatorio	Lavatory
Prohibido fumar	No Smoking
Prohibido escupir	No Spitting
Prohibido el estacionamiento	No Parking
Prohibida la entrada *or* Prohibido el paso	Keep Out
Abierto	Open
Cerrado	Closed
Entrada	Entrance
Salida	Exit

INTERNATIONAL ROAD SIGNS

DANGER

DANGER

MAIN ROAD AHEAD

CAUTION

SHARP TURN

RIGHT CURVE

LEFT CURVE

TAKE EITHER ROUTE

CROSSROAD

THIS WAY

DO NOT ENTER

FIRST-AID STATION

**GUARDED RAIL-
ROAD CROSSING**

**UNGUARDED RAIL-
ROAD CROSSING**

NO WAITING

NO PARKING

PARKING

NO VEHICLES

NO MOTOR VEHICLES

WEIGHT LIMIT 5½ TONS

**NO ANIMAL-
DRAWN TRAFFIC**

SPEED LIMIT

**OPEN CULVERT
(DIP)**

89

Monastery, El Escorial

ALPHABETICAL
WORD LIST

A

English	Pronunciation	Spanish Spelling
accelerator	ah-sel-ay-ra-DOR	acelerador
address	dee-reks-YOAN	dirección
admiral	ahl-mee-RAHN-tay	almirante
afternoon	TAR-day	tarde
again	O-tra VESS	otra vez
airport	ah-ay-ro-PWAYR-to	aeropuerto
airplane	ahv-YOAN	avión
alcohol, rubbing	ahl-KOAL day fro-TAR	alcohol de frotar
altitude	ahl-TOO-ra	altura
ambulance	ahm-boo-LAHNSS-ya	ambulancia
ammonia	ah-moan-YA-ko	amoníaco
ankle	to-BEE-yo	tobillo
answer	rresp-WEST-ah	respuesta
apples	mahn-SA-nahss	manzanas
April	ah-BREEL	abril
arm	BRA-so	brazo

English	Pronunciation	Spanish Spelling
armor	bleen-DA-hay	blindaje
aspirin	ah-spee-REE-na	aspirina
August	ah-GO-sto	agosto
auto	OUT-o	auto

B

English	Pronunciation	Spanish Spelling
back (*of person*)	ess-PAHL-da	espalda
bad	MA-lo	malo
baggage room	SA-la day	sala de equipajes
baked	ECH-o ahl OR-no	hecho al horno
bananas	ba-NA-noass	bananos
bandage	VEN-da	venda
barber	bar-BAY-ro	barbero
bathhouse	KA-sa day BAHN-yoass	casa de baños
beans	free-HO-less	frijoles
bed	KA-ma	cama
bedding	RRO-p'a day KA-ma	ropa de cama
beef	KAR-nay day VA-ka	carne de vaca
beer	sayr-VESS-ah	cerveza

English	Pronunciation	Spanish Spelling
beets	rrem-o-LA-cha	remolacha
belt	seen-too-ROAN	cinturón
better	may-HOR	mejor
bicycle	bee-see-KLET-ah	bicicleta
black	NEG-ro	negro
blades, razor	O-hahss day ah-fay-TAR	hojas de afeitar
blanket	fra-SA-da	frazada
bleeding	SAHN-gray	sangre
blouse	gay-RRAY-ra	guerrera
blue	ah-SOOL	azul
boat	BO-tay	bote
boiled	ko-SEED-o	cocido
book	LEE-bro	libro
bottom (of river)	FOAND-o	fondo
brake fluid	LEE-kee-do pa-ra FREN-oass	líquido para frenos
brakes	FREN-oass	frenos
brandy	BRAHN-dee	brandy
bread	PAHN	pan
bridge	PWEN-tay	puente
bridle	BREE-da	brida
broiled	ah-SA-do	asado

English	Pronunciation	Spanish Spelling
brown	PARD-o	pardo
brush	say-PEE-yo	cepillo
bulb, light (*electric*)	boam-BEE-ya	bombilla
burro	BOO-rro	burro
bus	out-o-BOOSS	autobús
bus station	est-ahss-YOAN del out-o-BOOSS	estación del autobús
butter	mahn-tay-KEE-ya	mantequilla
buttons	bo-TOAN-ess	botones

C

cabbage	KOAL	col
cable	KA-blay	cable
cablegram	ka-bleg-RA-ma	cablegrama
camel	ka-MAY-yo	camello
camp	kahm-pa-MENT-o	campamento
candy	DOOL-sess	dulces
car	OUT-o	auto
carburetor	kar-boo-ra-DOR	carburador
careful	kwee-DA-do	cuidado
carefully	koan kwee-DA-do	con cuidado

94

English	Pronunciation	Spanish Spelling
central	sen-TRAHL	central
certainly	say-GOO-ro	seguro
chains	ka-DEN-ahss	cadenas
chauffeur	cho-FAYR	chofer
cheaper	mahs ba-RA-to	más barato
cheese	KESS-o	queso
cherries	say-RESS-ahss	cerezas
chest	PECH-o	pecho
chicken	PO-yo	pollo
chief	HEF-ay	jefe
chocolate	cho-ko-LA-tay	chocolate
cigarette	see-ga-RREE-yo	cigarrillo
city	s‿yoo-DA	ciudad
clams	ahl-MAY-hahss	almejas
cleaned, dry	leemp-YAR	limpiar
clerk	esk-reeb-YEN-tay	escribiente
cloth	TEL-ah	tela
clutch	em-BRA-gay	embrague
coal	kar-BOAN	carbón
Coast Guard	el sayr-VEESS-yo day gwar-da-KO-stahss	El servicio de guardacostas

English	Pronunciation	Spanish Spelling
coat	cha-KET-ah	chaqueta
coconuts	KO-koass	cocos
coffee	ka-FAY	café
color	ko-LOR	color
comb	PAY‿ee-nay	peine
company	koam-pahn-YEE-ah	compañía
controls	MAHN-doass	mandos
cook	ko-see-NAY-ro	cocinero
correct	ek-SAHK-to	exacto
cotton	ahl-go-DOAN	algodón
cream	KREM-ah	crema
cup	TA-sa	taza
current	korr-YEN-tay	corriente

D

danger	pay-LEE-gro	peligro
dates	DA-tee-less	dátiles
dawn	ah-ma-nay-SAYR	amanecer
day	DEE-ah	día
December	deess-YEM-bray	diciembre
deck	koob-YAYR-ta	cubierta
deep	pro-FOOND-o	profundo

English	Pronunciation	Spanish Spelling
dentist	den-TEE-sta	dentista
detours	des-VEE-oass	desvíos
Diesel oil	ah-SAYT-ay D⌣YESS-el	aceite Diesel
direction	dee-reks-YOAN	dirección
disinfectant	dess-een-fek-TAHN-tay	desinfectante
doctor	MED-ee-ko	médico
driver	cho-FAYR	chofer
drug store	bo-TEE-ka	botica
dry	SEK-o	seco
dusk	oab-skoo-ray-SAYR	obscurecer

E

ear	o-RAY-ha	oreja
east	EST-ay	este
eggs	WEV-oass	huevos
elbow	KOAD-o	codo
electrician	el-ek-tree-SEE-sta	electricista
elevation, field	KO-ta	cota

English	Pronunciation	Spanish Spelling
engine	MA-kee-na	máquina
engine oil	ah-SAYT-ay day MA-kee-na	aceite de máquina
engineer	ma-kee-NEE-sta	maquinista
envelopes	SO-bress	sobres
equipment	ay-KEE-po	equipo
evening	NO-chay	noche
extinguisher, fire	est-een-TOR day een-SEND-yoass	extintor de incendios
eye	O-ho	ojo

F

face	KA-ra	cara
family	fa-MEEL-ya	familia
far	LAY-hoass	lejos
father	PA-dray	padre
February	feb-RAY-ro	febrero
filling station	soor-tee-DOR day ga-so-LEE-na	surtidor de gasolina

English	Pronunciation	Spanish Spelling
firearm	AR-ma day FWEG-o	arma de fuego
fireman	fo-go-NAY-ro	fogonero
firewood	LEN-ya	leña
first-aid packet	BOAL-sa day koo-rahss-YOAN	bolsa de curación
fish	pess-KA-do	pescado
flag	bahn-DAY-ra	bandera
flagship	BOO-kay een-SEEG-nee-ah	buque insignia
flashlight	leen-TAYR-na ay-LEK-tree-ka	linterna eléctrica
flat	YA-no	llano
flight (*aviation*)	seks-YOAN	sección
food	ko-MEE-da	comida
	or ah-lee-MENT-o	alimento
foot	P‿YAY	pie
fords	VA-doass	vados
fork	ten-ay-DOR	tenedor
fragile	FRA-heel	frágil
Friday	V‿YAYR-ness	viernes
fried	FREET-o	frito

English	Pronunciation	Spanish Spelling
friends	ah-MEE-goass	amigos
fuel tank	TAHN-kay day koam-boo-STEE-blay	tanque de combustible

G

English	Pronunciation	Spanish Spelling
garage	ga-RA-hay	garaje
gas	GAHSS	gas
gasoline	ga-so-LEE-na	gasolina
glaciers	ay-LAY-roass	heleros
glass	VA-so	vaso
gloves	GWAHN-tess	guantes
goggles	ahn-tay-O-hoass day ka-MEE-no	anteojos de camino
good	BWEN-o	bueno
good-by	ahd-YOASS	adiós
grapes	OO-vahss	uvas
gravel	GRA-va	grava
gray	GREESS	gris
grease	GRA-sa	grasa
green	VAYR-day	verde

English	Pronunciation	Spanish Spelling
grocery	bo-DEG-ah	bodega
group	GROO-po	grupo
guide	GHEE-ah	guía
guideposts	PO-stess een-dee-ka-DOR-ess	postes indicadores

H

hammer	mar-TEE-yo	martillo
hand	MA-no	mano
handkerchiefs	pahn-yoo-EL-oass	pañuelos
hat	soam-BRAY-ro	sombrero
head	ka-BESS-ah	cabeza
heavy	pay-SA-do	pesado
hello	O-la	hola
help	ah-YOO-da	ayuda
here	ah-KEE	aquí
high	AHLT-o	alto
hills	SAY-rroass	cerros
hip	ka-DAY-ra	cadera
horn	bo-SEE-na	bocina
horse	ka-BA-yo	caballo

English	Pronunciation	Spanish Spelling
horseshoe	ay-rra-DOO-ra	herradura
hot	kahl-YEN-tay	caliente
hotel	o-TEL	hotel
hour	O-ra	hora
how	KO-mo	cómo
husband	ma-REED-o	marido

English	Pronunciation	Spanish Spelling
ice	YEL-o	hielo
impassable	eem-pa-SA-blay	impasable
	or een-trahn-see-TA-blay	intransitable
ink	TEEN-ta	tinta
insecticide	een-sek-tee-SEE-da	insecticida
instruments	een-stroo-MEN-toass	instrumentos
interpreter	een-TAYR-pret-ay	intérprete
iodine	YO-do	yodo
iron		
corrugated iron	CHA-pa oan-doo-LA-da	chapa ondulada
sheet iron	YAY-rro en PLAHN-chahss	hierro en planchas

English	Pronunciation	Spanish Spelling

J

English	Pronunciation	Spanish Spelling
jack	GA-to	gato
January	ay-NAY-ro	enero
jaw	kee-HA-da	quijada
July	HOOL-yo	julio
June	HOON-yo	junio

K

key	YA-vay	llave
kilometer	kee-LO-met-ro	kilómetro
knee	rro-DEE-ya	rodilla
knife	koo-CHEE-yo	cuchillo

L

ladder	ess-ka-LAY-ra day MA-no	escalera de mano
lakes	LA-goass	lagos
lamb	kor-DAY-ro	cordero
languages	eed-YO-mahss	idiomas
large	GRAN-day	grande

English	Pronunciation	Spanish Spelling
larger	ma-YOR	mayor
laxative	lahk-SAHN-tay	laxante
left	eesk-YAYR-da	izquierda
leg	P_YAYR-na	pierna
lemons	lee-MO-ness	limones
lentils	len-TAY-hahss	lentejas
lettuce	lay-CHOO-ga	lechuga
light	LOOSS	luz
light (*weight*)	leev-YA-no	liviano
load	PESS-o	peso
lobster	lahn-GO-sta	langosta
long	LAR-go	largo
low	BA-ho	bajo
lumber	ma-DAY-ra	madera

M

Madam	sen-YO-ra	señora
mail	ko-rresp-oan-DENSS-ya	correspondencia

English	Pronunciation	Spanish Spelling
mangoes	MAHN-goass	mangos
many	MOO-choass	muchos
map	MA-pa	mapa
	or KRO-keess	croquis
	or PLA-no	plano
March	MAR-so	marzo
matches	FO-sfo-ro	fósforo
May	MA-yo	mayo
maybe	kee-SAHSS	quizás
meat	KAR-nay	carne
mechanic	may-KA-nee-ko	mecánico
medium	med-YA-no	mediano
men	OAM-bress	hombres
message	men-SA-hay	mensaje
	or rray-KA-do	recado
message center	SEN-tro day trahn-smeess-YO-ness	centro de transmisiones
messenger	men-sa-HAY-ro	mensajero
meters	MET-roass	metros
midnight	MED-ya NO-chay	media noche
milk	LECH-ay	leche

English	Pronunciation	Spanish Spelling
Miss	sen-yo-REE-ta	señorita
Monday	LOO-ness	lunes
money	dee-NAY-ro	dinero
month	MESS	mes
more	MAHSS	más
morning	mahn-YA-na	mañana
mother	MA-dray	madre
motor	mo-TOR	motor
motorcycles	mo-to-see-KLET-ahss	motocicletas
mountains	moan-TAHN-yahss	montañas
mouth	BO-ka	boca
movie	SEE-nay	cine
Mr.	sen-YOR	señor
Mrs.	sen-YO-ra	señora
muddy	fahn-GO-so	fangoso
mud puddles	CHAR-koass	charcos
mule	MOO-lo	mulo

N

nails	KLA-voass	clavos

English	Pronunciation	Spanish Spelling
narrow	ahn-GO-sto	angosto
nationality	nahss-yo-na-lee-DA	nacionalidad
Navy	lar-MA-da	La armada
near	SAYR-ka	cerca
nearest	mahss sayr-KA-no	más cercano
neck	KWAY-yo	cuello
needle	ah-GOO-ha	aguja
night	NO-chay	noche
no	NO	no
noon	med-yo-DEE-ah	mediodía
north	NOR-tay	norte
northeast	no-REST-ay	noreste
northwest	nor-o-EST-ay	noroeste
nose	na-REESS	nariz
November	noav-YEM-bray	noviembre
number	NOO-may-ro	número
nurse	en-fayr-MAY-ra	enfermera

English	Pronunciation	Spanish Spelling
	O	
observer	oab-sayr-va-DOR	observador
obstructions	oab-strooks-YO-ness	obstrucciones
October	oak-TOO-bray	octubre
oil	ah-SAYT-ay	aceite
Diesel oil	ah-SAYT-ay D⌐YESS-el	aceite Diesel
engine oil	ah-SAYT-ay day MA-kee-na	aceite de máquina
oil rating	EEN-dee-say day ah-SAYT-ay	índice de aceite
oil viscosity	vee-sko-see-DA del ah-SAYT-ay	viscosidad del aceite
switchboard operator	tel-ef-o-NEE-sta	telefonista
orange (*color*)	na-RAHN-ha	naranja
oranges	na-RAHN-hahss	naranjas
Ordnance Department	la ma-ay-STRAHN-sa	La maestranza
outfit	oo-nee-DA	unidad
overcoat	so-bray-TOAD-o	sobretodo

English	Pronunciation	Spanish Spelling

P

English	Pronunciation	Spanish Spelling
pants	pahn-ta-LO-ness	pantalones
paper	pa-PEL	papel
passable	pa-SA-blay	pasable
passes	PA-soass	pasos
paths	vay-RED-ahss	veredas
patrol	pa-TROO-ya	patrulla
peaches	mel-o-ko-TOAN-ess	melocotones
pears	PAY-rahss	peras
pencil	LA-peess	lápiz
pepper	peem-YEN-ta	pimienta
perishable	pay-ress-ay-DAY-ro	perecedero
pick	PEE-ko	pico
pigeon	pa-LO-ma	paloma
pillow	ahl-mo-AH-da	almohada
pilot	pee-LOAT-o	piloto
pineapples	PEEN-yahss	piñas
pins	ahl-fee-LAY-ress	alfileres
pistol	pee-STO-la	pistola
place	loo-GAR	lugar

English	Pronunciation	Spanish Spelling
plane	ahv-YOAN	avión
plate	PLA-to	plato
please	por fa-VOR	por favor
pliers	ah-lee-KA-tess	alicates
plums	seer-WEL-ahss	ciruelas
police	po-lee-SEE-ah	policía
Military Police	la po-lee-SEE-ah mee-lee-TAR	La policía militar
police station	kwar-TEL day po-lee-SEE-ah	cuartel de policía
pontoons	poan-TOAN-ess	pontones
pork	SAYRD-o	cerdo
porter	MO-so	mozo
postage	frahn-KAY-o	franqueo
post office	ko-RRAY-o	correo
potatoes	PA-pahss	papas
power plant	PLAHN-ta ay-LEK-tree-ka	planta eléctrica
private	soal-DA-do	soldado
propeller	EL-ee-say	hélice
pump	BOAM-ba	bomba
purple	mo-RA-do	morado

English	Pronunciation	Spanish Spelling

Q

questions	pray-GOON-tahss	preguntas
quick *or* quickly	RRA-pee-do	rapido
quinine	kee-NEE-na	quinina

R

radio set	ah-pa-RA-to day RRAHD-yo	aparato de radio
radio station	est-ahss-YOAN day RRAHD-yo	estación de radio
railroad	fay-rro-ka-RREEL	ferrocarril
raincoat	eem-payr-may-AH-blay	impermeable
raw	KROO-do	crudo
razor	na-VA-ha day ah-fay-TAR	navaja de afeitar
razor blades	O-hahss day ah-fay-TAR	hojas de afeitar
receipt	rray-SEE-bo	recibo
red	RRO-ho	rojo

111

English	Pronunciation	Spanish Spelling
reflector	rref-lek-TOR	reflector
region	rrehh-YOAN	región
repairs	rrep-ah-rahss-YO-ness	reparaciones
restaurant	rrest-ow-RAHN-tay	restaurante
rice	ah-RROASS	arroz
rifle	foo-SEEL	fusil
rifleman	foo-see-LAY-ro	fusilero
right	day-RECH-ah	derecha
river	RREE-o	río
road	ka-MEE-no	camino
rocky	ped-ray-GO-so	pedregoso
room	KWART-o	cuarto
rope	SO-ga	soga
rough	ahk-see-den-TA-do	accidentado
runway	PEE-sta	pista
ruts	rro-DA-dahss	rodadas

S

saddle	SEE-ya	silla

English	Pronunciation	Spanish Spelling
sand	ah-REN-ah	arena
sandy	ah-ray-NO-so	arenoso
Saturday	SA-ba-do	sábado
scarf	boo-FAHN-da	bufanda
scissors	tee-HAY-rahss	tijeras
scout	esp-lo-ra-DOR	explorador
screwdriver	dest-or-nee-ya-DOR	destornillador
seaman	ma-ree-NAY-ro	marinero
sedative	sed-ah-TEE-vo	sedativo
September	sept-YEM-bray	septiembre
several	VAR-yoass	varios
shaving cream	KREM-ah day ah-fay-TAR	crema de afeitar
sheets	SA-ba-nahss	sábanas
ship		
cargo ship	BOO-kay day KAR-ga	buque de carga
transport ship	trahn-SPOR-tay	transporte
shirt	ka-MEE-sa	camisa
shoelaces	kor-DOAN-ess day sa-PA-toass	cordones de zapatos
shoes	sa-PA-toass	zapatos
short	KORT-o	corto

English	Pronunciation	Spanish Spelling
sir	sen-YOR	señor
sketch	KRO-keess	croquis
sleigh	tree-NAY-o	trineo
slow *or* slowly	dess-PAHSS-yo	despacio
small	pay-KEN-yo	pequeño
snowdrifts	ven-tee-SKAY-roass	ventisqueros
soap	ha-BOAN	jabón
socks	kahl-say-TEE-ness	calcetines
soldiers	soal-DA-doass	soldados
soon	PROANT-o	pronto
soup	SO-pa	sopa
south	SOOR	sur
southeast	sood-EST-ay	sudeste
southwest	sood-o-EST-ay	sudoeste
spark plugs	boo-HEE-ahss	bujías
specialty	esp-ess-ya-lee-DA	especialidad
speed limit	vel-o-see-DA per-mee-TEE-da	velocidad permitida
spinach	esp-ee-NA-kahss	espinacas
splints	ta-BLEE-yahss	tablillas
spoon	koo-CHA-ra	cuchara

English	Pronunciation	Spanish Spelling
springs, (*of water*)	ma-nahnt-YA-less	manantiales
squash	ka-la-BA-sa	calabaza
stable	KWA-dra	cuadra
stamps	SAY-yoass	sellos
station	est-ahss-YOAN	estación
bus station	est-ahss-YOAN del out-o-BOOSS	estación del autobús
filling station	soor-tee-DOR day ga-so-LEE-na	surtidor de gasolina
steak	beef-TEK	biftec
stimulant	est-ee-moo-LAHN-tay	estimulante
stoker	fo-go-NAY-ro	fogonero
stomach	ess-TOAM-ah-go	estómago
strawberries	FRESS-ahss	fresas
strong points	POON-toass FWAYR-tess	puntos fuertes
submarine	soob-ma-REE-no	submarino
sugar	ah-SOO-kar	azúcar
Sunday	do-MEEN-go	domingo
sunglasses	GA-fahss ow-MA-dahss	gafas ahumadas
sweater	SWET-ayr	sweater
swift	RRA-pee-da	rápida

English	Pronunciation	Spanish Spelling
	T	
tail	KO-la	cola
tailor	SA-stray	sastre
tan	ka-NEL-ah	canela
taxi	TAHK-see	taxi
tea	TAY	té
telegram	tel-eg-RA-ma	telegrama
telephone	tay-LEF-o-no	teléfono
telephone lines	LEE-nay-ahss tel-ay-FO-nee-kahss	líneas telefónicas
tent	T⌐YEN-da	tienda
thank you	GRAHSS-yahss	gracias
there	ah-YEE	allí
things	KO-sahss	cosas
thread	EE-lo	hilo
throat	gar-GAHN-ta	garganta
Thursday	HWEV-ess	jueves
ticket	bee-YET-ay	billete
ticket office	ta-KEE-ya	taquilla

English	Pronunciation	Spanish Spelling
timetable	ee-tee-nay-RAR-yo	itinerario
tire	nay-oo-MA-teé-ko	neumático
tire patches	PAR-chess day nay-oo-MA-tee-ko	parches de neumático
today	OY	hoy
toilet	esk-oo-SA-do	excusado
toilet paper	pa-PEL eeh-YEN-ee-ko	papel higiénico
tomatoes	to-MA-tess	tomates
tomorrow	mahn-YA-na	mañana
tooth	say-PEE-yo	muela
toothbrush	say-PEE-yo day D_YEN-tess	cepillo de dientes
toothpaste	PA-sta den-TEE-free-ka	pasta dentífrica
tooth powder	POAL-voass den-TEE-free-koass	polvos dentífricos
tourniquet	tor-nee-KET-ay	torniquete
towel	to-AH-ya	toalla
town	PWEB-lo	pueblo
	or po-BLA-do	poblado
train	TREN	tren
truck	kahm-YOAN	camión

117

English	Pronunciation	Spanish Spelling
truth	vayr-DA	verdad
tube, inner	KA-ma-ra day ba-LOAN	cámara de balón
	or TOO-bo een-tayr-YOR	tubo interior
Tuesday	MAR-tess	martes
turnips	NA-boass	nabos

U

underwear	RRO-pa een-tayr-YOR	ropa interior
uniforms	oo-nee-FOR-mess	uniformes
urgent	oor-HEN-tay	urgente
U. S. Consulate	koan-soo-LA-do day loass ess-TA-doass oo-NEE-doass	consulado de los Estados Unidos
U. S. Government	goab-YAYR-no day ess-TA-doass oo-NEE-doass	gobierno de Estados Unidos

V

value	va-LOR	valor
vegetables	lay-GOOM-bress	legumbres
very	MOO‿ee	muy

English	Pronunciation	Spanish Spelling
viscosity	vee-sko-see-DA	viscosidad
visibility	vee-see-bee-lee-DA	visibilidad

W

English	Pronunciation	Spanish Spelling
wagon	KA-rro	carro
water	AH-gwa	agua
watermelon	sahn-DEE-ah	sandía
Wednesday	M‿YAYR-ko-less	miércoles
week	say-MA-na	semana
well (*for water*)	ahl-GOON PO-so	algún pozo
well (*good*)	B‿YEN	bien
west	o-EST-ay	oeste
wet	OO-med-o	húmedo
white	BLAHN-ko	blanco
wife	ess-PO-sa	esposa
wind	V‿YENT-o	viento
wind direction	dee-reks-YOAN del V‿YENT-o	dirección del viento
wind velocity	vel-o-see-DA del V‿YENT-o	velocidad del viento

English	Pronunciation	Spanish Spelling
wine	VEE-no	vino
wings	AH-lahss	alas
wire	ah-LAHM-bray	alambre
wire cutters	kor-ta-LAHM-bray	cortaalambre
woods	BO-skess	bosques
wound	ay-REE-da	herida
wounded	ay-REE-do	herido
wrench	YA-vay een-GLESS-ah	llave inglesa

Y

years	AHN-yoass	años
yellow	ah-ma-REE-yo	amarillo
yes	SEE	sí
yesterday	ah-YAYR	ayer

Convent of San Esteban, Salamanca

Gateway into Judios District, Cordoba